Railways

Althea and Edward Parker

Illustrations by Peter Kent

Contents

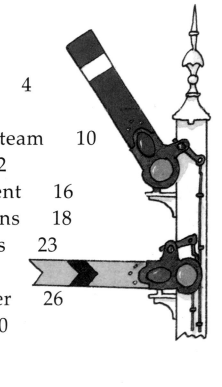

A & C Black · London

Beginnings

Railways are one of the very few examples of a technology that began, in a way, by accident rather than by design.

Long before the Romans started building stone-paved roads, cart wheels made ruts in the roadways and these were filled in with broken stone to make a hard surface for the wheels. This made the carts easier to pull and the wheels packed the stone down into solid tracks.

This is a lot easier than pulling it through the mud.

Wheels dug into soft ground, forming ruts, which were filled in with small stones.

Stone rut-ways were carved in rocky tracks.

The main thing about these early tracks was that it was an easy way to make a hard road which saved having to pull carts over rough ground. The fact that the wheels were guided by the ruts was not important at this stage. About 2500 years ago, the Greeks developed this idea by carving deep grooves into cart tracks worn naturally into rocky roads. These rut-ways became quite modern looking, with crossing points and sidings. They not only made the carts easy to pull, but also stopped them falling over the edge of mountain tracks.

When the Romans began building networks of hard, paved roads, carts could be pulled much more easily. Since there wasn't any particular need for rut-guided wheels, railways didn't progress much further for several hundred years.

The Romans built proper stone-paved roads so their armies could march quickly from place to place.

Wheels and tracks

Miners had a hard and often dangerous job pushing heavy trucks through low, narrow tunnels, mostly in pitch darkness.

Modern railways began in mines in about the middle of the 14th Century. They were used to move heavy trucks full of coal or metal ores through narrow tunnels.

The miners wanted a surface which made it easier to push the carts and also needed a way of stopping the carts from banging into the walls of the tunnels. It was also useful to have a road surface that could be easily extended as the mine got bigger, or taken up and used elsewhere when the mine was closed.

These mine railways had a track made of two heavy wooden planks with a narrow gap between them. The waggons had ordinary wheels, with a guide-pin on the front axle. The pin ran in the gap between the planks and kept the wheels on the track. The miners discovered that the wheels wore grooves in the planks. At first, this was thought of as a nuisance because the planks had to be replaced or turned over. In fact what was happening was that the rut-way had been re-invented.

The flange on the inside of both wheels kept them from rolling off the track and guided the trucks around corners.

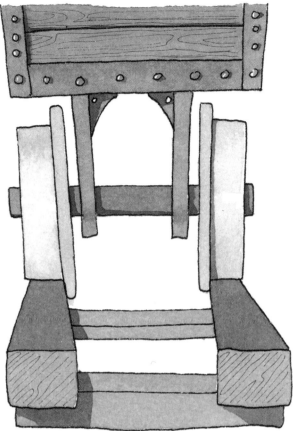

The guide-pin fitted into the gap between the planks.

Model racing cars also use a guide-pin to keep the cars on the track.

The next step was to make the rut the means of guiding the wheels, but the really clever thing that was done was to put the guide in the wheel instead of the track. The tracks were made of narrower pieces of wood and the wheels were made with a bit of the rim sticking out. This is called a flange and it kept the wheels on the track.

The track began to look like heavy pieces of ladder. It had cross pieces to keep the tracks the right distance apart and was pegged to the ground or packed down with broken stones to keep it in place.

Later, the wooden tracks often had iron bars nailed to them to make them more hard-wearing. These were used until 1767 when the first iron rails were cast. Iron rails, and the iron wheels which were then fitted to the waggons, were a great improvement on wood because they were stronger and did not need repairing so often. But the biggest advance was that they reduced friction. Horses were able to pull twice as much on smooth iron rails as they could on rough wooden ones.

I can push lots of rabbits on the smooth, slippery ice.

At about this time, two types of railway track were being tried out. One was the edge rail with a flat-topped rail and flanged wheel and the other was the plate or tram-way, which had the flange on the rail instead of the wheel.

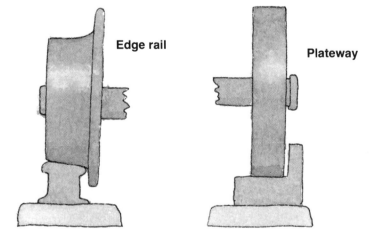

Edge rail

Plateway

6

An Irish train had wheels in the middle and ran on a single rail. If too many passengers got in one side, the train fell off the track.

The plateway was thought to have an advantage because the waggons, which had ordinary wheels, could be pulled over ordinary roads. But it was not as strong as the edge rail. Stones and dirt also collected on the rail, which made the waggons more difficult to pull. One way of getting over this problem was to make the wheel rim very narrow to cut through the dirt, but this meant the waggons could not be used on roads.

Although a number of plateways were built, the edge rail proved to be a much better design and became the standard kind of track throughout the world.

Early railways

Trials had proved that a horse could pull a load about ten times heavier on a railway than it could on a road and, by the early 18th Century, extensive networks of horse-drawn railways were in use in many parts of the world. Since railways developed as a part of mine workings, the biggest ones at first were around mines and linked them with the local town and river.

In 1801, a public horse railway was built between Croydon and Wandsworth in south London, England. This was followed soon after by a line built between Linz in Austria and Ceské Budějovice in Czechoslovakia. This was the longest line in Europe and carried barrels of salt from the mines to barges on the River Danube.

This horse-drawn railway is taking goods to the river where they will be loaded on to barges. The passengers are riding in stage-coach bodies fixed to railway wheels.

As the advantages of railways over poor roads became more obvious, longer and longer lines were built between more towns and villages. Slow, heavy freight trains and fast passenger trains, pulled by teams of horses, were soon running regular services.

The railway companies operated their tracks like toll roads and anybody could pay to run trains on them. This caused chaos and made it almost impossible to keep to any timetables because each train ran whenever its owner wanted it to run. This sometimes made for terrible arguments when two trains met in the middle of a stretch of single-line track. Everything was held up while each driver tried to persuade the other to back his train up to the nearest crossing point.

I got to the middle first. You'll have to back up.

Stop arguing and get moving. I've got a ship to catch.

9

Experiments with steam

Railways had two main advantages over roads. They were cheaper to build because they were narrower and the foundations used less material. They also made it possible to pull several waggons at a time. At the beginning of the 19th Century, people were starting to think in terms of a nation-wide network of railways and looking for alternatives to horse power. Horses needed lots of food, they had to rest, they were expensive to buy and a lot of them were needed to run a railway. Steam power seemed a possible alternative to horses.

Pulleys are wheels with a groove around the edge to take a rope or a chain. As the ropes moved around the pulley wheels, they pulled the railway trucks along the track.

Steam engines used for pumping water out of mines were adapted for pulling trucks on railways.

Steam engines had been invented 100 years earlier and were used mainly for pumping water out of mines. These pumping engines were too big and heavy to move along on a railway track but experiments were carried out to pull trains with engines fixed in once place. Engines were placed at intervals along the track and drove pulleys connected to a continuous loop of rope. The waggons were hitched to the rope and pulled along. These rope railways were often used to pull loaded waggons up steep slopes.

They will never replace horses you know.

The cable cars in San Francisco are pulled along by moving cables set into the surface of the road. They work in the same way as the early railways, which were pulled by moving ropes.

Smaller engines were also being developed. These used steam at a higher pressure than the mine engines and could be made light and small enough to run on a track. They produced enough power to drive themselves and a train of waggons. They were clumsy machines but worked in the same way as a modern steam engine.

PICK-UP TRAINS

In the 1890s, the British Army in India had portable railways. The engines, carriages and track could be carried across mountains on the backs of elephants and re-laid somewhere else.

Steam engines

Steam engines produce power by allowing steam at high pressure to expand inside a cylinder and push a piston. Steam is a gas, and a hot gas, at a high pressure, will expand as it drops to a lower pressure. The expansion produces a force which can be used to do useful work.

In a steam engine, a fire heats water in a boiler. This turns the water into high-pressure steam, which is taken by pipes to a cylinder. A piston is free to slide up and down inside the cylinder, like a bicycle pump. The steam is fed in behind the piston, forcing it to the other end of the cylinder where the steam escapes or 'exhausts' to the outside air.

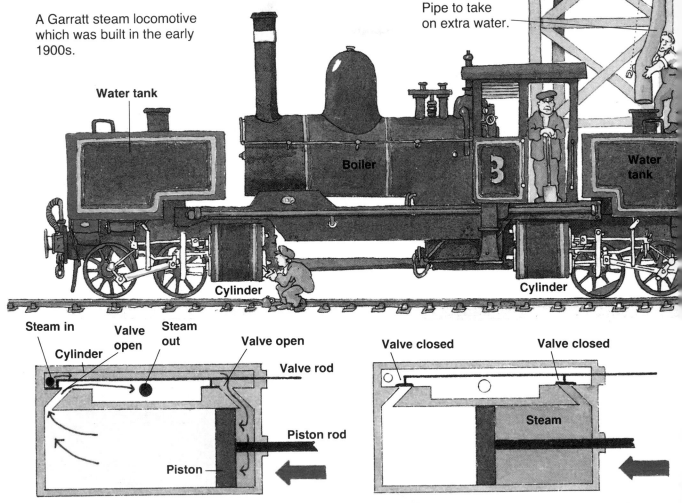

Water tower

Pipe to take on extra water.

A Garratt steam locomotive which was built in the early 1900s.

Water tank

Boiler

Water tank

Cylinder

Cylinder

Steam in · **Valve open** · **Steam out** · **Valve open** · **Valve rod**

Cylinder

Piston rod

Piston

1 Hot steam from the boiler is starting to push one side of the piston.

Valve closed · **Valve closed**

Steam

2 The steam expands, pushing the piston down the cylinder. This is the 'power stroke'.

Valves in the cylinder then let steam in behind the other side of the piston forcing it back to the other end of the cylinder where the steam exhausts again. This process is repeated continuously with the valves letting steam in to one side of the piston and then the other.

The piston, which is being driven backwards and forwards in the cylinder, drives a piston rod which is connected to the driving wheels through a crank. This turns the to-and-fro movement of the piston into the round and round movement of the wheels. The piston rod is guided by slide-ways, which keep it in a straight line.

A British steam engine on the Great Eastern Railway in 1909.

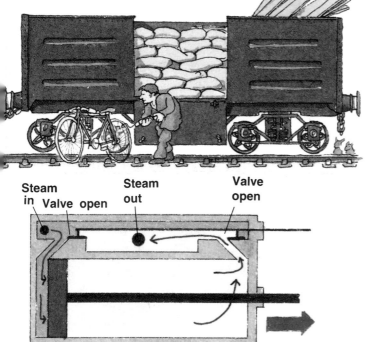

Steam in **Valve open** **Steam out** **Valve open**

3 Hot steam from the boiler is starting to push the other side of the piston so it will move back up the cylinder again.

STICKY PORRIDGE

Holes in leaking steam engines were often plugged with oatmeal. Sometimes this soaked up water and turned to porridge, blocking the engine completely.

The Penydarran steam engine, which was used in Wales, Britain, in the 18th Century.

At least horses don't knock your head off.

A partly successful steam engine ran on the Penydarran mine railway in Wales. This engine had one cylinder built inside the boiler with the piston rod sticking out of the front. This drove the wheels through a long connecting rod and crank. It was a fearfully dangerous machine to drive because the levers which controlled the steam valves were out in front of the piston rod. The driver had to walk ahead of the engine and stood a good chance of having his head knocked off by the moving piston rod.

The engine had a very simple boiler. It was a large drum with the fire burning in a tube or 'flue' which ran through the middle. The flue turned upwards at the end of the boiler and became the chimney.

14

The Penydarran engine was too heavy for the weak cast-iron rails and broke up the track as it went. Also, because it had an inefficient boiler, it used up a lot of coal and was much more expensive to run than horses. It did prove though, that a steam engine could pull heavy loads over a railway track.

After the Penydarran engine, several designs were tried out. Most of them worked reasonably well but none were good enough to convince railway owners that steam could completely replace horses. For some time, railways were built to use horse power.

TRAIN WITH LEGS

A walking engine, invented in 1815, managed a speed of 3.2 kilometres an hour. But it destroyed the track and exploded.

George Stephenson's *Locomotion No 1*, built for the Stockton and Darlington Railway.

William Hedley's *Puffing Billy*, built for the Wylam Colliery Railway.

The locomotive *Atlantic*, which ran on the Baltimore and Ohio Railroad.

The Delaware and Hudson's *DeWhitt Clinton* pulling a train of stage coaches.

Railway development

The design of steam engines was improving all the time. In 1829, the owners of the newly-opened Liverpool and Manchester railway held trials at Rainhill in England to decide on the type of engines they were going to use on their railway. They laid down stiff rules but several engine-builders entered their engines.

An engine called *Rocket*, built by George Stephenson, won the trials. It was successful because it had a multi-tube boiler which was a better design than earlier engines. The hot gases from the firebox went through a series of small tubes instead of one large tube. The *Rocket's* boiler could raise more steam with far better fuel economy than any other engine of the time.

The *Rocket*, *Novelty*, and *Sans pareil* competed at Rainhill, England for a prize of £500. The *Rocket* proved that steam engines were a better choice than horses.

16

The *Rocket's* type of engine became the prototype for all engines that followed. After a similar contest on the Baltimore and Ohio railway in America, steam locomotives were used on most railways throughout the world. Horse power virtually died out, although not completely. Charlie, the last known railway horse, retired in 1967 from shunting trucks on British Railways.

Huge viaducts are now so much a feature of the landscape that people think of them almost as natural features. It is unlikely that huge motorways will ever be thought of in the same way.

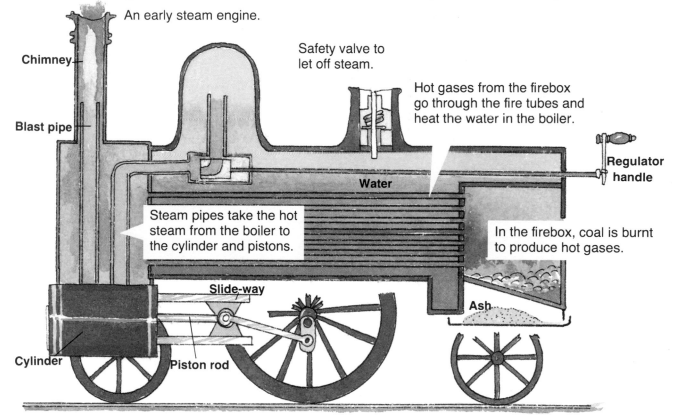

An early steam engine.

Chimney

Blast pipe

Cylinder

Piston rod

Slide-way

Safety valve to let off steam.

Hot gases from the firebox go through the fire tubes and heat the water in the boiler.

Regulator handle

Water

Steam pipes take the hot steam from the boiler to the cylinder and pistons.

In the firebox, coal is burnt to produce hot gases.

Ash

The development of steam railways bought about improvements in track design as heavier and longer trains increased the wear on the tracks. Stronger steel rails replaced the earlier, and weaker, cast-iron rails. Railways crossed rivers and valleys on huge brick viaducts and went through mountains in tunnels dug with pick-axes and shovels. The railway 'navvies' were the highest-paid workers of their day and many of the bridges and viaducts they built are carrying trains far heavier and faster than the early railway builders dreamed of.

17

Controlling the trains

Stop the trains! There's been another crash. It's chaos up there.

Faster and more frequent trains also brought about improvements in methods of working the railway, particularly as passenger traffic increased and the consequences of accidents became more serious.

When trains were still being pulled by horses, at speeds not much above walking pace, signalling could be a fairly casual affair. Although there were accidents, they were usually not very serious. The introduction of steam engines brought trains weighing hundreds of tonnes and travelling at 50, 60 or even 80 kilometres per hour. It became important to have some method of controlling the trains so that they didn't run into each other.

EXPLODING SIGNAL

Someone suggested that the guard could hurl a smouldering bag of gunpowder towards the driver. The explosion would warn the driver to slow down. The idea didn't catch on.

Trains were first controlled by the time interval system. This sounds pretty terrifying by modern standards and relied on a policeman, as the first signalmen were called. The policeman would check the time as a train went by and stop the next train if less than a certain amount of time had passed, often only five minutes. When the time was up, he would let the next train go.

This was fine as long as the first train hadn't broken down further up the line. This often happened, so the next train ran into the back of the one in front. There were many accidents where a policeman passed train after train at five minute intervals before a bruised and breathless fireman arrived to warn him of the destruction further up the line.

The invention of the electric telegraph introduced a new and much better method of controlling trains called the 'space interval' or 'block' system.

The electric telegraph was the forerunner of the telephone and worked in a similar way. Instead of a microphone and ear-piece, the electric current in the telegraph wires worked a pointer on a dial in each telegraph machine.

With the telegraph, the railway was divided up into lengths or blocks, with a telegraph machine at the end of each block. The signalman could set the pointer on his machine which would set the pointer on the next machine down the line. Each signalman would then know, by the pointer being set to 'train on line' or 'train in block', that he shouldn't let a train go until the next signalman had cleared the line by setting his pointer to 'line clear'. This made sure that two trains could not be on the same stretch of track at the same time and that they were a safe distance apart.

Early types of semaphore signals that could be swivelled around to show go or stop.

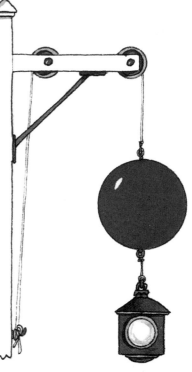

A signal where different coloured balls could be hoisted up a flagpole to warn the engine driver of danger ahead.

Even with the block system, accidents still happened because it relied on engine drivers obeying the signals. At first, these were often only hand signals or flags waved by the signalman. Frequently, engine drivers didn't see them and drove their train into a block which already had another train in it. Signals quickly improved though and standard semaphore signals were introduced, with coloured lights for night work.

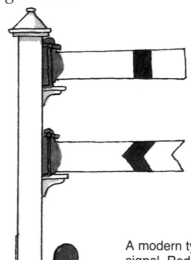

Common types of semaphore signals which showed straight out for stop and up for go.

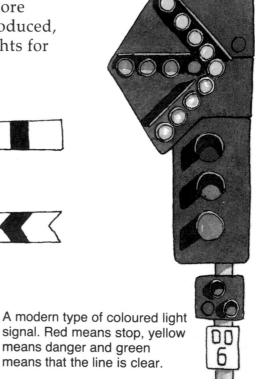

A modern type of coloured light signal. Red means stop, yellow means danger and green means that the line is clear.

Levers to change the signals.

The older signal boxes, which had big brass levers to operate the signals, have been replaced by control rooms full of electronic equipment. Modern signalling and train control systems use electronics and computers to keep a check on the positions of the trains. Signals are now usually coloured light systems, like traffic lights. The most modern railway systems have built-in safety devices such as 'automatic train control'. This is a mechanism on the track which automatically puts on the train brakes if the driver mistakenly passes a stop signal.

A modern signal box where computers are used to record the positions of the trains on the tracks.

Underground trains

On some railway systems, such as the London underground or 'tube', the Paris metro and the New York subway, the trains control their own signals. There are switches on the track, operated by the train's wheels, which set the last signal to stop as the train enters each block.

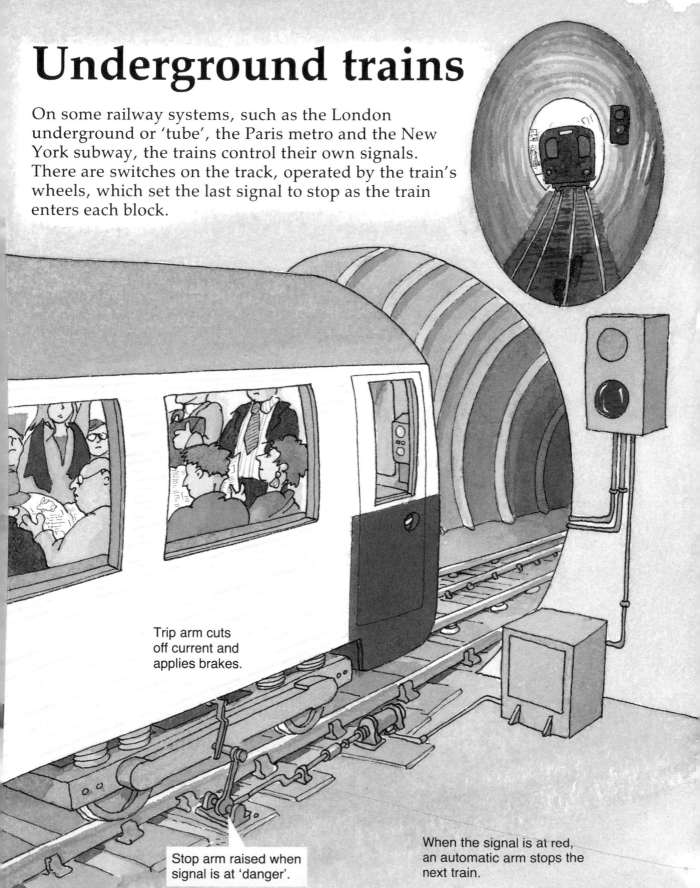

Trip arm cuts off current and applies brakes.

Stop arm raised when signal is at 'danger'.

When the signal is at red, an automatic arm stops the next train.

Passengers

Travel on early railways was often uncomfortable, cold and dirty. In early trains, 1st class passengers had stage-coach carriages, made from road carriages mounted on railway wheels. The cheaper classes of carriage were very basic and 3rd class passengers had to put up with open waggons more like cattle trucks. They sometimes did not even have seats. There were cases of passengers actually freezing to death in open carriages and railway companies soon realized that they had to look after their passengers better. Carriage design improved rapidly and things like steam heating, lighting and toilets were introduced for 1st and 2nd class passengers. Eventually even 3rd class passengers could travel in reasonable comfort.

The modern French train in the background is a 'double decker', with an upstairs deck. Each carriage can carry twice as many people as an ordinary railway carriage.

One of the major advances in passenger comfort and safety was the improvement of train brakes. Early train brakes were very primitive; often the only brake was on the engine. As carriage design improved, trains were fitted with continuous brakes in which every wheel in the train was braked. The engine driver was able to bring the whole train smoothly and quickly to a stop. If any of the couplings between the carriages broke, these brakes came on automatically.

When communication cords were first introduced, passengers would use them for all sorts of silly reasons, such as if a hat blew out of the window.

Second and third class passengers travelled in primitive conditions on the early railways.

In the early days, the passengers had no way of warning the driver if something was wrong. Later, a cord was strung along the carriages and connected to a bell on the engine. This 'communication cord' was not very successful because the driver found it difficult to hear the bell above the noise of the engine. In modern trains, the communication cord is usually a valve, connected to the brakes, which passengers can pull in an emergency to stop the train.

New forms of power

Now, just as steam replaced the horse, steam has been replaced by other forms of power. But, despite the fact that it died out thirty years ago, steam has been so much a part of railway history that road level crossings in some countries still have signs showing a steam engine.

Electricity was tried out very early on. In 1842, a battery-powered engine ran in Scotland and, in 1885, an electric locomotive was tried out on the New York elevated railway. This was very popular at the time because people walking under the railway used to complain about hot coals from the steam engines falling on their heads. The first main line electrified railway ran on the Baltimore and Ohio railway in America, and a line from Hungary through the Simplon tunnel to Italy was electrified in 1906.

I'm glad I don't have to sit on a steam engine.

Ouch! It's like walking under a coal fire.

This small-scale electric locomotive ran at the Berlin exhibition in 1879. It picked up power from a third rail laid down the middle of the track.

An early electric locomotive on the Baltimore and Ohio Railway in America.

Electricity is supplied to the locomotives through power cables over the tracks or a third rail beside the track. The locomotives draw their power from a 'pick-up shoe' which slides along the cable or along the third rail. Many railway engineers were suspicious of electricity because the engines had to rely on power produced somewhere else. It was thought to be better for the train to have an engine producing its own power. Because of this, diesel engines became the first main alternative to steam engines.

A British electric locomotive picking up electricity from power cables strung above the track.

The most common sort of diesel engines use a combination of diesel and electric power. They have a big diesel engine driving an electric generator, which in turn supplies power to electric motors driving the wheels. This system combines the advantage of a self-contained engine with the smoothness of electric power.

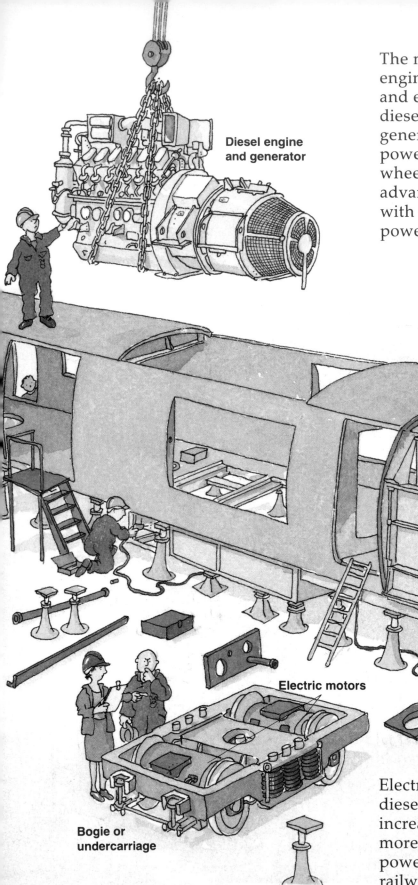

Diesel engine and generator

Electric motors

Bogie or undercarriage

Electric power is now replacing diesel because the cost of oil fuel has increased to a point where it is now more economical to burn the fuel in power stations rather than in the railway engines.

Governments and railway companies are trying hard to encourage more people to use the railways for carrying heavy freight. Railways have the advantage over roads of being able to move very heavy loads with the smallest possible engine power. A one thousand tonne train needs an engine developing about 2240 kilowatts (3000 horsepower). To move the same weight on the road takes a fleet of 33 trucks with about twice the same combined engine power. The train therefore uses fuel more efficiently. Railways also take up less space than a six-lane highway. Because of this, they cause less damage to our environment than road transport.

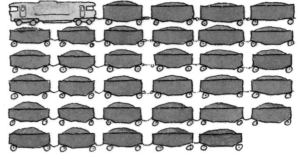

1 train pulls 1000 tonnes

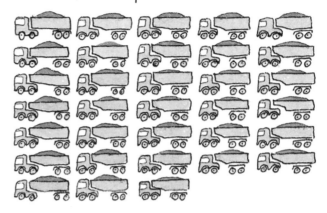

33 trucks pull 1000 tonnes

The French TGV cruises at 250 kilometres per hour.

The Japanese train called the *Tokaido* travels nearly as fast as a jumbo jet as it zooms along the line between Tokyo and Osaka. It has been nicknamed the 'bullet' train because it is so fast.

Into the future

Before the networks of motorways and roads were built, railways carried most of the world's heavy goods and freight overland. And, when air travel was not as commonplace as it is now, trains were the main way of going long distances across countries and continents.

An American passenger locomotive of the 1930s.

Some trains were very luxurious. The *Orient Express*, which ran from Paris to Istanbul, was like a travelling hotel and was the most comfortable way to travel – if you could afford it. Royalty travelled around in trains fitted out like luxury houses with proper beds, bathrooms and sitting rooms furnished with sofas, desks and even telephones. Some trains had observation cars and upper-deck lounges which made the journey itself very exciting.

Luxury train

Royal coach

Observation car

Railway networks throughout the world opened up land that could not easily be reached in any other way. Whole new towns sprang up around railway stations. The American city of Chicago became a big town because it was built up around the railway which bought beef cattle in from the plains of South Dakota and Colorado to the cattle markets.

It is quite possible that in the next century railways will again become as important as they were a hundred years ago, particularly for moving very heavy or bulky goods such as cars or big machines. At the moment, railways are the best way of moving bulk materials, such as coal, across countries. A lot of work is going into developing integrated transport systems. In these, railways carry goods long distances and then they are unloaded into road trucks for local deliveries. This will reduce the need to build more roads, which are expensive and damage the environment.

Index

First published 1992
A & C Black (Publishers) Limited, 35 Bedford Row, London, WC1R 4JH

ISBN 0-7136-3533-9

© 1992, text, Althea and Edward Parker
© 1992, illustrations, Peter Kent

A CIP catalogue record for this book is available from the British Library.

Acknowledgements
Edited by Barbara Taylor
Photographs by: Alan Cork pages 11, 24; Mary Evans Picture Library page 13; British Rail pages 17, 27; British Railways Board 22; French Railways (Lafontant) page 29.

Filmset by Rowland Phototypesetting Limited
Bury St Edmunds, Suffolk
Printed in Italy by L.E.G.O. Spa.